We Love the New York Giants

Jokes About Our Rivals

Copyright

Version 1

This book is a joke book, written in a light hearted way.

No offence is meant to any person or group of people

Read, laugh and enjoy a joke

Introduction

Thank you for taking the time to read this book. In this book we take a light hearted look at football and our rivals.

We have scoured the country for some of the best and funniest jokes, most jokes were thought up at the stadium or in the bar after a game and a few beers.

This book covers some of the best jokes; no joke has been kept out of this book for being politically incorrect or too rude.

Get ready to share a laugh at our rival's expense.

A fellow walks into a restaurant, orders a drink, and asks the waiter if he'd like to hear a good Notre Dame joke. "Listen buddy," he growled. "See those 2 big guys on your left? They were both linemen on the Notre Dame football team. And that huge fellow on your right was a world-class wrestler at Notre Dame. That guy in the corner was Notre Dame's all-time champion weight lifter. And I lettered in 3 sports at Notre Dame. Now, are you absolutely positive you want to go ahead and tell your joke here?" "Nah, guess not," the man replied. "I wouldn't want to have to explain it 5 times

What do you get when you put 28 Arkansas cheerleaders in one room?

A full set of teeth

Bloke comes home from the bar drunk at 4am in the morning. His wife is sleeping and he tries to sneak into bed. He's laying in bed for a few minutes and lets rip a fart. His wife wakes up and asks, "What in the world was that?" He replies, "Touchdown, I'm up 7 nothing." She thinks to herself, "I'm gonna fix him." Then she lets one loose. He yells at her, "What was that?" She replies "Touchdown, tie score." Now he thinks, "I'm gonna fix her." He's laying there for about 10 minutes trying to work one up. He tries so hard he craps in bed. The wife asks, "Now what in the world was that?" He replied, "Half time, switch sides."

A guy took his girlfriend to her first football game. Afterward he asked her how she liked the game. "I liked it, but I couldn't understand why they were killing each other for 25 cents," she said. "What do you mean?" he asked. "Well, everyone kept yelling, 'Get the quarter back!"

Why did the Nebraska line backer steal a police car?

He saw "911" on the side and thought it was a Porsche.

Why did god invent football?

So that married men could have some physical contact in their lives.

Where do hungry football players play?

In the Supper Bowl

Which football team cooks gourmet meals together?

The Kansas City Chefs

Which player is the easiest target to hit with the football?

The wide receiver

What did the football say to the punter?

"I get a kick out of you"

What end does the quarterback look at before the ball is hiked?

The rear end

What football player has very strong legs and builds houses?

A car-punter

Did you here about the football player who asked his coach to flood the field so he could go in as a sub?

Where do quarterbacks go when they get old?

Out to pass-ture

What do you call a lineman's kids?

Chips off the old blocker

What football player should you be suspicious of?

The quarterback sneak

What did the football coach say to the broken vending machine?

"Give me my quarterback!"

What should you put in the end zone to keep the other team away?

A scorecrow

Why do coaches like punters?

Because punters always put their best foot forward

What's the difference between a sofa and a man watching Monday Night Football?

The sofa doesn't keep asking for beer

I've heard that Australian football is a lot rougher than the American version, but never believed it until I witnessed a game first hand.

In the first half, I saw 3 broken arms, half a dozen sprains, and at least 4 broken noses. That was just the cheerleaders.

List of insulting nicknames for all NFL Teams:

Bears:
Bores, Dancing Bears

Bengals:
Ben-Gays, Bungles, Bungholes

Bills:
Biles, Belles, Duffalo, Barffalo, Doug & The Slugs, Rob's Johnsons, Wade's Wads, Jills

Broncos:
Donkeys, Pony Boys, Griese Monkeys, Shanahan's Sham, Orange Crushed, Donkos, Doinks, Pack Mules

Browns:

Dawgs, Hounds, Mutts, Hershey Squirts, Sh*t Stains, Clowns, Blowns

Buccaneers:

Tampon Bay, Suckaneers, Yuckaneers

Cardinals:

Canaries, Cadavers

Chargers:

Bolts, Dolts, Discharges, Charburgers, San Di-yecch-o, Cryin' Ryans, Sparklers, Light Bulbs

Chiefs:

Chefs, Cheaps, Chokes, Cheeps, Chimps, Squaws, Thiefs, Chumps,
 Queefs, Cheeks, Kansas Shitty, Cheats

Colts:

Indianapolis .500, Ponies, Dolts, Geldings, Mules

Cowboys:

Dal-loss, Cowgirls, Cowchips, Cryboys, Cokeboys, Cowboobs, Dull-Ass, Chokeboys, Cowdogs, Dal-last

Dolphins:

Fins, Cryami, Tuna, Fish, Dullfins, Guppies, Bait, Chum

Eagles:

Filthydelphia, Pigeons, Chickens, Turkeys, Beagles

Falcons:

Geese, Ducks, Silver & Blecch, Buzzards, Dirty Birds, Shitty Birds

49ers:

San Fagcisco, The Village People, 69ers, Farty Whiners, FortyNinnies

Jaguars:

Jagoffs, Jagwads, Jagwhores, Jackasses, Faguars, Michael Jacksonville

Jets:

Gliders, Paper Airplanes, Jerks, Gits, Swamp Gas, Jesters

Lions:

Lie-downs, Loins, Cowardly Lions

Packers:

Velveetas, Fudge-Packers, Ass-Packers, The Cheez, Slackers

Panthers:

Pussycats, Pussies, Kittens

Patriots:

Patsies, Tea Men, Spats, Patties, Pattycakes

Raiders:

Chokeland, Fraiders, 'Roiders, Faders, Afraiders, Masqueraiders, Traitors, Gayders, RaiDuhs

Rams:

Lambs, Scrams, Sheep

Ravens:

Modell's 'Mos, Crows

Redskins:

Foreskins, Deadskins, Greenskins

Saints:

Ain'ts, New Whoreleans, Simps, Faints, Quaints, French Ticklers, The SuperDumb, Shanks.

Seahawks:

Seachickens, Water Chickens, Seacocks, Seahags, Chickenhawks, Seahacks, Seatwats, Seaducks, Semenhawks, Seasquawks, Weakhawks, Chicks, Winged Water Rats, Shithawks, Seafags, Seahonks, Seagulls

Steelers:

Curtain Rods, Cowher's Cowards, Kordell & The Pride Parade, squealers, Armpitsburgh, Stillers, Cellars

Titans:

Titanics, Titties

Vikings:

Viqueens, Swedish Chefs, Purple Peepee Eaters

St. Peter was manning the Pearly Gates when 40 Eagles fans showed up. Never having seen a Eagles fan at heaven's door, St. Peter said he would have to check with God. After hearing the news, God instructed him to admit the 10 most virtuous from the group.

A few minutes later, Saint Peter returned to God breathless and said, "They're gone."
"What? All of the Eagles fans are gone?" asked God.
"No" replied Saint Peter "The Pearly Gates!"

How many Philadelphia Eagles does it take to win a Super Bowl?

Nobody knows and we may never find out

Why shouldn't Eagles fans be worried about the Eagles recent layoffs?

They were all defensive players so no one will ever notice

What is the difference between a Cowboys fan and a coconut? One's thick and hairy and the others a tropical fruit

Three old football fans are in a church, praying for their teams.

The first one asks, "Oh lord, when will we get to the Super Bowl?" God replies "In two years' time"

"But I will be dead by then", said the old man.

The second fan asks "When will we next win the Super Bowl?"

"In ten years' time", God replies

But I'll be dead by then, said the old man

The last man asks "When will the Eagles win the Super Bowl?"

God thinks and then says "I will be dead by then"

Rumor has it that to cut the cost of the repairs to the Jets scoreboard, only the light bulbs in the half used to show the opponents score will be fixed.

The other half will just have 'NY Jets 0' painted on in yellow paint.

The Eagles are apparently under investigation by the IRS for tax evasion; they've been claiming for Silver Polish for the past 10 years.

What's the difference between a female Eagles fan and a pit bull?

Lipstick

There was once a fanatical Giants fan who thought of nothing but football all day long. He talked about football, read about football, watched nothing but football on television and attended games as often as he possibly could.

Finally his poor wife could not stand it any longer. One night she said, 'I honestly believe you love the Giants more than you love me!'

'Gosh,' said the fan, 'I love the Jets more than I love you!'

I've started watching the Jets, as my doctor says I should avoid any excitement.

Top tip for Cowboys fans: don't waste money on expensive new jerseys every season.

Simply strap a large inflatable penis to your forehead, and everyone will immediately know which team you support.

One of the highest paid players in the NFL, John had everything going for him. He had an expensive new mansion, a new sports car, a wardrobe full of designer clothes.

His only problem was that he had three girlfriends and he couldn't decide which one to marry. So he decided to give $5,000 to each woman to see what she would do with it.

The first woman bought new clothes for herself and had an expensive new hairdo, a massage, facial, manicure and pedicure.

The second woman bought a top-of-the range DVD and CD player, as well as an expensive set of golf clubs and tennis racquet and gave them all to John. "I used the money to buy you these gifts because I love you," she told him.

The third woman invested the money in the stock market, and within a short time had doubled her investment. She gave John back the initial $5,000 and reinvested the profit. "I'm investing in our future because I love you so much," she said.

John considered carefully how each woman had spent the money, and then married the woman with the biggest breasts.

A quarterback had had a particularly bad season and announced that he was retiring from professional football. In a television interview he was asked his reasons for quitting the game.

'Well, basically,' he said, 'it's a question of illness and fatigue.'

'Can you be more specific?' asked the interviewer.

'Well,' said the player, 'specifically the fans are sick and tired of me.

A woman goes to see the doctor.

"Doctor, doctor, I'm very worried about my son," she said. "All he does is play football all day; then he comes in covered in mud and walks all over my clean carpet."

"I think you may be over-reacting," said the doctor reassuringly. "Sons often behave like that"

"I know, doctor," said the woman, "but it's not just me that's worried about him. His wife is too"

My wife told me last week that she'd leave me if I didn't stop spending so much time at football games.

'What a shame!'

'Yes. I shall miss her'

A woman was reading a newspaper one morning and said to her husband,

'Look at this, dear. There's an article here about a man who traded his wife for a season ticket to the Giants. You wouldn't do a thing like that, would you?'

'Of course I wouldn't!' replied her husband. 'The season's almost over!'

Snow White arrived home one evening to find her home destroyed by fire. She was especially worried because she'd left all seven dwarves asleep inside. As she scrambled among the wreckage, frantically calling their names, suddenly she heard the cry: "The Jets for the Super Bowl."

"Thank goodness," sobbed Snow White. "At least Dopey's still alive!"

The ASPCA have acted swiftly after recent results.

If you see any Eagles fans walking a dog please call them immediately on 0-6 0-12 0-18 0-24 as they're not very good at holding on to leads

Four surgeons are taking a coffee break:

1st surgeon says "Accountants are the best to operate on because when you open them up, everything inside is numbered"

2nd surgeon says "Nope, librarians are the best. Everything inside them is in alphabetical order"

3rd surgeon says "Well you should try electricians. Everything inside them is color coded"

4th surgeon says "I prefer Eagles fans. They're heartless, spineless, gutless and their heads and butts are interchangeable"

How do you change a Cowboys fans mind?

Blow in his ear!

What's the difference between a Eagles fan and a broken clock?

Even a broken clock is right twice a day

What's the difference between a Jets fan and a coconut?

You can get a drink out of a coconut

Two guys were walking through a cemetery when they see a tombstone that read: "Here lies John Smith, a good man and a Eagles fan"

So, one of them asked the other: "When the hell did they start putting two people in one grave?"

Two Eagles fans jump off a cliff. Which one hits the ground first?

Who gives a F**k!

What do you get when you cross an Eagles fan with a pig?

I don't know, there are some things a pig just won't do

What do you call a Eagles fan on the moon?

A Problem

What do you call 100 Eagles fans on the moon?

A. An even bigger problem

What do you call all the Eagles fans on the moon?

Problem solved

How do you define 199 Cowboys fans

Gross Stupidity

Why do Eagles fans whistle whilst sitting on the john?

So they know which end to wipe

What's the difference between an Eagles fan and an Onion?

No one cries when you chop up an Eagles fan!

Did you hear that the postal service just recalled their latest stamps?

They had photos of Cowboys players on them, people couldn't figure out which side to spit on.

How many Eagles fans does it take to pave a driveway?

Depends how thin you slice them

What would you call a pregnant Eagles fan?

A dope carrier

What do you call an Eagles fan with half a brain?

Gifted

What do Eagles fans use as birth control?

Their personalities

How many Eagles supporters does it take to stop a moving Bus?

Never enough

What do you call a Cowboys fan with no arms and legs?

Trustworthy

What's the difference between a dead dog in the road and a dead Eagles fan?

Skid marks in front of the dog

What's the difference between an Eagles fan and a Vibrator?

An Eagles fan is a real dick

If you see a Eagles fan on a bicycle, why should you never swerve and hit him?

You don't want to damage your bike

What would you call two Eagles fans going over a cliff in an SUV?

A complete waste of space. You could have squeezed six of them into one of those.

What's the difference between an Eagles fan and a bucket of crap?

The bucket

How do you get a one armed Cowboys fan down from a tree?

Wave at him

How do you keep a Redskins fan busy?

Put him in a round room and tell him to sit in the corner

What do Eagles fans and mushrooms have in common?

They both sit in the dark and feed on nothing but crap

How many Eagles fans does it take to change a light bulb?

It doesn't matter, because they're all condemned to eternal darkness

Rex Ryan was going to the Jets Halloween party dressed as a pumpkin

But at midnight he still hadn't turned into a coach

How is a pint of milk different than an Eagles fan?

If you leave the milk out for a week it develops a culture

What's the difference between an Eagles fan and a sperm?

At least a sperm has one chance in 5 million of becoming a human being

There's a rumor going about that if you buy a season ticket at the Lincoln Financial Field then you get a free space suit.

Apparently it's due to the lack of atmosphere

How do you save an Eagles fan from drowning?

Take your foot off his head

What's the difference between a busload of Eagles fans and a Hedgehog?

On a hedgehog, the pricks are on the outside

What do Hemorrhoids and Cowboys fans have in common?

They're both a complete pain in the ass and never seem to go away completely

Why did the Redskins fan climb the glass window?

To see what was on the other side

What's the difference between a Redskins fan and a Chimp?

One's hairy, stupid and smells, and the other is a chimpanzee

An anxious woman goes to her doctor. "Doctor," she asks nervously, "I'm a bit worried - can you get pregnant from anal intercourse?"

"Of course," replies the doctor, "Where do you think Eagles fans come from?"

How do you kill an Eagles fan when he's been drinking?

Slam the toilet seat on his head

What's the difference between Pamela Anderson and the Eagles Quarterback?

Pam's only got two tits in front of her

Santa Claus, the tooth fairy, an intelligent Cowboys supporter and an old bum are walking down the street together when simultaneously they each spot a fifty dollar bill. Who gets it?

The old bum of course. The other three are mythical creatures.

How can you tell a level headed Cowboys fan?

He dribbles from both sides of his mouth - at the same time

Newsflash

Thieves broke into the home of a Cowboys fan and stole two books. "The thing that upsets me", he said "is that I hadn't finished coloring them in yet!"

What do you get if you cross a Monkey with an Eagles fan?

Nothing. Monkeys are far too clever to screw an Eagles fan

What is the difference between a battery and a Jets fan?

A battery has a positive side

What's the difference between the Jets defense and a taxi driver?

A taxi driver will only let in four at a time

What do Eagles fans and laxatives have in common?

They both irritate the crap out of you

What's the ideal weight for an Eagles fan?

Three pounds, that's including the Urn

Two Cowboys fans are on the plane on the way to a game

One turns to the other and says "Hey John! If this plane turns upside-down will we fall out?"

"No way Steve," says his friend "of course we'll still be pals!"

You're trapped in a room with a Lion, a snake and an Eagles fan. You have a gun with two bullets. What should you do?

Shoot the Eagles fan, twice

What do you call a Cowboys fan in a suit?

The accused

Why did God make Eagles fans smelly?

So blind people could laugh at them too

What do you call 100 Eagles fans at the bottom of a cliff?

A good start

What do you call a dead Cowboys fan in a closet?

Last year's winner of the hide and seek contest

What do you call a Cowboys fan that does well on an IQ test?

A cheat

What has 120,000 arms and an IQ of 170

Lincoln Financial Field during every game

Why do people take an instant dislike to Eagles fans?

It saves time

What do you say to an Eagles fan with a job?

Can I have a Big Mac please

What do you get if you see a Cowboys fan buried up to his neck in sand?

More sand

What's the difference between a Cowboys fan and a shopping cart?

The cart has a mind of its own

A Cowboys fan goes to his doctor to find out what's wrong with him.

"Your problem is you're fat" says the doctor

"I'd like a second opinion" responds the man

"OK, you're ugly too" replies the doctor

A Giants and Eagles fan get into a nasty car accident. Both vehicles are really wrecked, but amazingly neither of them are hurt.

After they crawl out of their cars, the Giants fan says, "So you're an Eagles fan, that's interesting. I'm a Giants fan.

Wow! Just look at our cars. There's nothing left, but fortunately we are unhurt. This must be a sign from God that we should meet and be friends and live together in peace the rest of our days."

The Eagles fan replied, "I totally agree, this must be a sign from God!"

The Giants fan went on, "And look at this - here's another miracle. My car is completely demolished but this bottle of Jack Daniels didn't break. Surely God wants us to drink it, to celebrate the fact we are alive?"

He hands the bottle to the Eagles fan, who nods his head in agreement, opens it and takes few big swigs from the bottle, then hands it back to the Giants fan.

The Giants fan takes the bottle, immediately puts the cap back on, and hands it back to the Eagles fan. The Eagles fan asks, "Aren't you having any?"

The Giants fan replies, "Nah, I think I'll just wait for the cops"

A truck driver used to keep himself amused by scaring every Eagles fan he saw walking down the Street in their jersey. He would swerve as if to hit them, and at the last minute, swerve back onto the road.

One day as he was driving along the road, he saw a priest hitch-hiking. He thought he would do his good deed for the day and offer the priest a lift.

"Where are you going, Father?" he asked.
"I'm going to say mass"

"No problem," said the driver, "Jump in and I'll give you a ride"

The priest climbed into the truck and they set off down the road. Suddenly the driver sees an Eagles fan on the sidewalk, and instinctively swerved as if to hit him, but just in time, remembering the priest in his truck, swerved back to the road again, narrowly missing the idiot.

Although he was certain that he didn't hit him, he still heard a loud "Thud". Not understanding where the noise came from, he glanced in his mirrors, and, seeing nothing, said to the priest, "Oh sorry Father, I nearly hit that Eagles fan"

"No need to apologize Son," replied Father, "I got the ba*tard with the door!"

What's the difference between OJ Simpson and the Eagles?
OJ at least had a defense

What do they call a drug ring in Dallas?

A huddle

What's the difference between the Jets and Cheerios?

Cheerios belong in a bowl

Wanna hear a joke?

The Dallas Cowboys

What's the difference between a vacuum cleaner and the Dallas Cowboys?

There's only one dirt bag in a vacuum cleaner

What did the Eagles fan say after his team won the Super Bowl?

"Dammit mom, why'd you wake me up? I was having an amazing dream!"

How are the Eagles like my neighbors?
They can't pick up a single yard

Want to hear a Cowboys joke?
Tony Romo

Why is Tony Romo like a grizzly bear?
Every fall he goes into hibernation

What's the difference between the Eagles and a dollar bill?
You can still get four quarters out of a dollar bill

What do the Eagles and possums have in common?
Both play dead at home and get killed on the road

What is the difference between a Jets fan and a baby?

The baby will stop whining after a while

How many Eagles players does it take to change a tire?

One, unless it's a blowout, in which case they all show up

What do you call 53 millionaires around a TV watching the Super Bowl?

The Dallas Cowboys

What do the Dallas Cowboys and Billy Graham have in common?

They both can make 60,000 people stand up and yell "Jesus Christ"

How do you keep a Jets player out of your yard?
Put up goal posts

Why are so many Eagles players claiming they have swine flu?
So they don't have to touch the pigskin

How do you stop an Eagles fan from beating his wife?
Dress her in a Giants jersey

If you have a car containing a Cowboys wide receiver, a Cowboys linebacker, and a Cowboys defensive back, who is driving the car?
The cop

How do you castrate a Dallas Cowboys fan?
Kick his sister in the mouth

What should you do if you find three Eagles fans buried up to their neck in cement?

Get more cement

What's the difference between an Eagles fan and a carp?

One is a bottom-feeding, scum sucker, and the other is a fish

How did the Cowboys fan die from drinking milk?

The cow fell on him

What does an Eagles fan do when his team wins the Super Bowl?

He turns off the PlayStation

What do you call a Dallas Cowboy in the Super Bowl?

A referee

Did you hear that the Eagles football team doesn't have a website?

They can't string three "W's" together

What does an Eagles fan and a bottle of beer have in common?

They're both empty from the neck up

Why do Eagles fans keep their season tickets on their dashboards?

So they can park in handicap spaces

How do you keep an Eagles fan from masturbating?

You paint his dick in Giants colors and he won't be able to beat it any more

Why do the Cowboys want to change their name to the Dallas Tampons?

Because they are only good for one period and do not have a second string

What's the difference between the Eagles and the Taliban?

The Taliban has a running game

Where do you go in Dallas in case of a tornado?

Cowboys Stadium, they never get a touchdown there

Why do ducks fly over Cowboys Stadium upside down?

There's nothing worth crapping on

What do you call an Eagles player with a Super Bowl ring?

A thief

Terror Alert

The Eagles football practice was delayed for nearly three hours yesterday after a player reported finding an unknown white powdery substance on the practice field.

Practice was stopped and the cops and the FBI were called in. After a complete analysis, FBI forensic experts determined that the white substance unknown to these players was in fact the goal line. Practice resumed after Special Agents decided the team was unlikely to encounter the substance again this season.

There's a rumor that after the current sponsorship expires the Eagles have lined up a new sponsor, Tampax

They thought it was an appropriate change as the team is going through a very bad period.

Tony Romo just threw his iPhone in frustration but it was intercepted and returned for a touchdown.

What Does the Dallas Cowboys and the movie Broke Back Mountain have in common?

They both have cowboys that suck.

Why is Tony Romo unable to answer a telephone?

He can't find the receiver

Did you know the Cowboys had a 11 and 5 season this year?

11 arrests, 5 convictions

Why doesn't Arlington have a professional football team?

Because then Dallas would want one

After the game, Tony Romo threw his helmet towards the sideline in disgust and that too was intercepted.

Why was Ron Turner mad when the Bears playbook was stolen?

Because he hadn't finished coloring it

CPSIA information can be obtained at www.ICGtesting.com
Printed in the USA
BVOW04s0206191214

380148BV00001B/47/P